EXPERIENCE

THE GOSPEL OF

MARK

EXPERIENCE
SCRIPTURE

Experience Scripture is designed specifically to help students engage with God's Word through reading and reflection. It is our prayer that students will apply the principles revealed in Scripture as they seek to better understand God and His plan for their life.

More resources and information can be found by visitng www.xpscripture.com

 @xpscripture

HOW TO USE
EXPERIENCE SCRIPTURE

This book is designed to be a tool for you to use as you *Experience Scripture*. The Gospel of Mark is divided into 30 days of reading, learning, and experiencing. Use these step-by-step instructions to help understand how you can best use this tool.

KNOW BEFORE YOU GO:

This section explains the background information you need in order to understand the day's Scripture. In other words, it gives some ideas for you to know before you go and read.

READ THE PASSAGE:

The Scripture for the day's *Experience* will be listed on the top of the left page. Do not skip this reading! The goal of this book is to help you read and understand Scripture. This is the most important step in your *Experience*.

AFTER THE PASSAGE:

This section then explores the messages, themes, or confusing parts in the day's Scripture. It is not meant to be the "answer key" as we will not address every question or issue that you may have after reading Mark. The point is to introduce you to Scripture and help you understand the main idea, or bottom line, for each day.

EXPERIENCE:

This section creates space for you to process or *Experience* each day's Scripture. The questions are meant to engage different parts of your mind, so each day's *Experience* will vary in style. We want you to go beyond simply reading Mark. We want you to *Experience* its truth for yourself. Take time to respond to the questions provided and be honest with yourself as you *Experience Scripture*. Do not feel boxed in by the questions! Use this space to explore what God is teaching you.

[TAKEAWAY AND PRAY]:

This section prompts you to choose one personal application. Consider the ideas you have processed and commit one as your main takeaway. Then, focus your daily prayer on one specific request, confession, and/or praise. Naming this one specific prayer allows you to reflect on God's power and possible answer to prayer as time passes.

We are excited for you to Experience Scripture over the next 30 days!

WHO
IS JESUS?

This question, as popular as it is today, was even more common 2,000 years ago when Jesus walked the Earth. Confusion and controversy follow this Teacher from Bethlehem as He performs such amazing miracles and speaks with such confident authority. And while much of Jesus' teaching references familiar Old Testament passages and themes, He often draws to new, and even uncomfortable, conclusions. The Gospel of Mark records the events of Jesus' life, prompting future readers to ask the same question the crowds ask during ancient times, "Who is Jesus?"

AUTHOR:

Mark. Mark was known to be Peter's (Jesus' disciple) trusted assistant.

PURPOSE:

Mark provides a brief account of Jesus' time on Earth. He writes about Jesus' ministry, healings, teaching, death, and resurrection. He writes to show that Jesus is the Son of God and Savior of the world!

STYLE:

Fast-paced and action-packed. Mark rarely provides details or descriptive language: he gets right to the point!

KEY VERSE:

Mark 10:45

THEMES:

The Cost of Discipleship: Mark shows that while following Jesus may be costly, it is worth it.

Upside Down: Mark records Jesus' new, counter-cultural value system to mankind.

Son of God: Mark's portrayal of Jesus leaves no doubt that He is indeed the Son of God.

Heart over Rules: Mark emphasizes that Jesus' ultimate concern is the condition of our hearts.

Love and compassion: Mark highlights Jesus' love and compassion for the world through His miracles, teachings, and sacrifice.

MAJOR CHARACTERS:

Jesus: The controversial Jewish leader who claimed to be the Son of God.

Pharisees: Religious leaders who were experts in the Old Testament Law. Pharisees had a reputation for prioritizing rules over a genuine relationship with God.

The Disciples: A group of twelve men that Jesus chose to be His first followers. While they often misunderstood Jesus' words and actions, Jesus used this faithful group to advance His mission in incredible ways!

TERMS TO KNOW:

Miracles: Signs that show Jesus' power

Parables: Stories from everyday life that explain complicated truths

Gospel: The Good News of salvation, offered through Jesus' life, death, and resurrection

READ: # MARK
1:1-15

KNOW BEFORE YOU GO:

Mark explains how John the Baptist prepares people for Jesus' ministry on Earth.

AFTER THE PASSAGE:

The Gospel of Mark introduces us to Jesus' ministry; however, it begins with a reference to the Old Testament (Mark 1:1-3 is quoting Malachi 3:1 and Isaiah 40:3). Even though we often talk about the Bible as two different parts—the Old Testament and the New Testament—they are actually two parts of the same story. When we see Old Testament verses quoted in the New Testament (like Mark 1:2-3), they are a reminder that Jesus' life continues the story of God in the Old Testament.

Mark 1:1-3 also shows us that John the Baptist's calling is significant because the Old Testament mentions it is going to happen hundreds of years before John the Baptist is even born. So, try not to be fooled by his unique clothes and peculiar diet (Mark 1:6): he is actually an incredibly important person in the story of Jesus. John the Baptist is chosen by God to pave the way for Jesus and prepare people for the Good News they are about to hear (Mark 1:4-5). He is not some crazy guy walking around preaching a random sermon—he is specifically called by God to tell people about Jesus!

John's entire life purpose is to make sure that when Jesus arrives, people's hearts are ready to receive His message. Although John gains popularity and fame, he continues to use his platform to point others to Jesus. Think of how different this approach is from most celebrities! Typically, the more famous people get, the more people talk about themselves. John the Baptist does the exact opposite: he points others to Jesus (Mark 1:8). In fact, he is so determined to make sure people understand that Jesus is truly the one to worship, he tells the crowds that he is not even worthy to untie Jesus' sandal: the job of a slave in the time of Jesus (Mark 1:7). What incredible humility and a powerful example for us!

[THE BOTTOM LINE]

Our entire lives are meant to point others to Jesus.

EXPERIENCE

Complete this sentence: My life points other people to

As we see in John the Baptist's example, God wants our lives to point other people to Jesus. However, our gifts, our desires, and our relationships can get in the way of this calling. You may realize that your life actually points other people to things, hobbies, success, or even yourself instead of Jesus. Now, ask someone that you trust to complete the sentence for you. Sometimes others can view the results of our actions more clearly than we see them ourselves.

**How can your life point others to Jesus? Consider your gifts,
your friends, your family, and your time.**

[TAKEAWAY & PRAY]

MY PRAYER TODAY IS: ☐ *A REQUEST*   ☐ *A CONFESSION*   ☐ *A PRAISE*

MY TAKEAWAY:	MY PRAYER:

READ: **MARK**

1:16-20, 2:13-17, 3:13-19, 6:6-13

KNOW BEFORE YOU GO:

Jesus chooses His twelve disciples from all different backgrounds.

AFTER THE PASSAGE:

These select passages (we will come back to the passages we skipped in the coming days) describe the group of people that Jesus chooses as His first followers—the disciples. Perhaps the most extraordinary thing about Jesus' choice of men is these men are extremely *ordinary*. They are not rich, influential, famous, or religiously trained; they are just ordinary people.

In fact, one man that Jesus chooses causes quite a controversy—He calls a man named Levi who is a tax collector (Mark 2:14). Tax collectors are some of the most hated people in Jesus' day and under no circumstances do people think a person like Levi should be hanging around someone like Jesus. When Jesus is questioned about His choice, He tells the crowd He is not just interested in being around "nice" or "good" people (Mark 2:17). The main reason Jesus came to Earth is to be with sinful, rude, and even mean people. In this passage, Jesus introduces a new way of thinking that we will see throughout the Gospel of Mark: everyone needs a Savior. Jesus is going to use ordinary people to communicate this truth!

Though the disciples waste no time in following Jesus—some literally leave right in the middle of their jobs—Mark 6:6-13 shows this excitement is not just a spur of the moment decision. Well into Jesus' ministry, this group of ordinary men continue to follow Jesus—even if it means giving up everything (Mark 6:8-9). While certainly the disciples and their faith are not perfect, Jesus uses the faith and dedication of these men to do extraordinary things (Mark 6:12-13)!

[*THE BOTTOM LINE*] ————————————————

Jesus uses the ordinary to do the extraordinary.

EXPERIENCE

Even before Jesus chooses the disciples, God had a record of using the ordinary to display His power. For example, He uses Moses' ordinary staff to deliver Israel from Egypt, the most powerful nation in the world! God uses a slingshot in the hand of a teenager named David to defeat Goliath—one of the strongest, most feared warriors in history! In these circumstances, including the ministry of the disciples, it is not the power of the object, but rather God's power, that allows the ordinary to have extraordinary results.

List five things in your life that are very ordinary. Your list could include your school supplies, your chore list, your phone, or something in your house. We use these objects everyday in very ordinary ways. **Now, consider how God could use these things to do the extraordinary. List the possibilities next to your five ordinary things.** Let these items be a reminder that through God's power, God can, and does, use ordinary things in the hands of ordinary people to do the extraordinary.

ORDINARY ITEM	*EXTRAORDINARY POSSIBILITY*

[TAKEAWAY & PRAY]

MY PRAYER TODAY IS: ☐ *A REQUEST*   ☐ *A CONFESSION*   ☐ *A PRAISE*

MY TAKEAWAY:

MY PRAYER:

READ: **MARK** *1:21-45*

KNOW BEFORE YOU GO:

Jesus continues His ministry by miraculously healing people.

AFTER THE PASSAGE:

Jesus' way of teaching is different than the other teachers' way in His time. He speaks like He has words directly from God—and He does (Mark 1:21-22). In addition to His powerful teaching, Jesus catches people's attention with incredible miracles like the ones Mark describes in this passage.

Both Jesus' teachings and miracles show His *authority* over all things (Mark 1:27). This word, *authority*, is an important word to understand because it is used often in the Gospel of Mark. When a person has authority over something, the person has the power to make decisions or give orders. It is important to understand that authority is gained through having the correct *position* as well. For instance, if your math teacher, Mr. Smith, assigns you homework, then you understand that you should come to class tomorrow with your homework completed. Your teacher has the power, or authority, to give you that instruction. If, however, a math expert who is not your teacher asks you to complete a homework assignment, then you would be less motivated to finish the homework. Why? Because you understand that Mr. Smith's *position* as your teacher is what gives him the ability to assign you homework. It is not his knowledge of math or his ability to do math problems. Mr. Smith is the only person who has *authority* in this area of your life.

The same idea is true of Jesus. Jesus has authority because He is the Son of God. He is a good teacher and does incredible miracles, but His authority comes from God alone. The miracles in Mark 1:21-45 are important because they show Jesus' authority and power have no limits. He has authority over the spiritual world (driving out demons) and the physical world (Peter's mother-in law and the man with leprosy). There has never been, or will ever be, anyone like Jesus—His authority sets Him apart from all of history! He demonstrates this authority in these miracles and can exercise the same authority in your life as well.

[*THE BOTTOM LINE*] ———————————————

Jesus' authority has no limits.

EXPERIENCE

Sometimes when we think of authority, we think of it as a negative idea. Teachers assign work to students, children have to obey their parents, the law creates rules to follow, and so on. However, we see through Jesus' example that authority can actually bring about order, healing, and life change.

List the ways the following authority figures help your life.

Position	How can the following authority figures help you?	How is Jesus' authority similar or different of these people?
Teacher		
Coach		
Police Officer		
Referee		
President		

What parts of your life do you need to surrender to Jesus' authority?

[TAKEAWAY & PRAY]

MY PRAYER TODAY IS: ☐ *A REQUEST* ☐ *A CONFESSION* ☐ *A PRAISE*

MY TAKEAWAY:

MY PRAYER:

READ: # MARK
2:1-12

KNOW BEFORE YOU GO:

Jesus shows His authority when He both heals and forgives a paralyzed man.

AFTER THE PASSAGE:

Like the leper in the previous chapter, the paralyzed man has incredible faith that Jesus has the power to heal him. After a very dramatic entrance, Jesus says something that surprises, and frustrates, some people in attendance (Mark 2:6-7). Rather than heal the man immediately, Jesus tells the man that his sins are forgiven (Mark 2:5). What prompts Jesus to say this? Forgiveness is not what the man had come for—he wanted the ability to walk! Jesus offers this paralyzed man forgiveness for two reasons:

1 Our greatest need is spiritual, not physical. While this man certainly has a great physical need, Jesus' first priority is to forgive the man of his sins—to set his soul right with God. In other words, what good is it to walk *physically* if you are not walking *spiritually* with God?

2 Jesus is indeed God! Who else could offer such a bold thing as forgiveness? Perhaps there are others in the region that could heal people. While astounding, it most likely would not have been the first time this crowd saw a healing. The crowd had never heard someone speak on behalf of God like Jesus does. Jesus is clearly and directly telling the crowds that He is more than a prophet or a faith healer—He Himself is God walking on Earth (Mark 2:10-12)! We will see this theme develop in the coming days as we keep reading the Gospel of Mark together.

[THE BOTTOM LINE]

Our greatest need is for our soul to be right with God.

EXPERIENCE

List several basic human needs.

Look back at your list. How many of the needs listed are "physical" needs? Things like a house, health, or clothes? Why do you think it is easier for us to consider our physical needs before our spiritual needs?

In addition to things like clothes and food, we have spiritual and emotional needs. We all have a need to be loved by God and others. We need strength to get through hard times. We need courage to do the right thing. We need peace when life is stressful. While less obvious, our spiritual needs are just as real as our physical needs.

What spiritual need do you have today? Pray and ask God to meet this need.

[TAKEAWAY & PRAY]

MY PRAYER TODAY IS: ☐ A REQUEST ☐ A CONFESSION ☐ A PRAISE

MY TAKEAWAY:

MY PRAYER:

READ: **MARK**

2:18-2:28, 3:1-12, 3:20-34

KNOW BEFORE YOU GO:

We will be introduced to several religious laws and traditions from the Old Testament in these passages.

AFTER THE PASSAGE:

This group of passages can be a bit tricky to understand—fasting (Mark 2:18-20), garments and wineskins (Mark 2:21-22), the Sabbath and Abiathar the High Priest (Mark 2:23-28, 3:1-6), and Beelzebul and eternal sin (Mark 3:20-34)—what does it all mean? Without getting too overwhelmed by the details, let us consider the major themes and lessons in these passages.

The law from the Old Testament included rules for people to follow. For example, there were instructions about fasting: not eating for a period of time to show focus, commitment, and dedication to God (Mark 2:18-20). There were guidelines of what someone could do and not do on the Sabbath, God's holy day (Mark 2:23-28). These rules helped people understand who was following God and who was not—the rules were a few of the many ways that people interacted with God and were set apart from other religions.

But with Jesus and His Good News, everything changes! Jesus tells people the primary way to interact with God is now through a relationship with Jesus—not through a set of traditions, rules, and rituals. Jesus is trying to help the people understand that, while those rules were not bad or evil, the rules were never meant to be a substitute for a genuine relationship with God. Unfortunately, many religious leaders, called the Pharisees, prioritize following these rules over loving God.

[THE BOTTOM LINE] ———————————————————————

Rules, rituals, and traditions are no substitute for a genuine relationship with God.

EXPERIENCE

Find something in your house that you can easily and safely remove the batteries from—something like a flashlight or remote. With the batteries removed, try to turn on the object. Any luck? Of course not—the batteries are removed! Now put the batteries back in and try again—everything works, right?

It does not make sense for you to use a remote without batteries—it will not work. It also does not make sense to do religious things without a real relationship with Jesus. The Pharisees' rules and traditions, like fasting, are like a remote control without the batteries. Their actions are not bad—they are just pointless unless they extend from a real love for God.

How can you avoid acting like a Pharisee in your relationship with God?

What types of actions are a temptation for you to do without a real relationship with God?

How can you use actions to actually draw near to God?

[*TAKEAWAY & PRAY*]

MY PRAYER TODAY IS: ☐ A REQUEST ☐ A CONFESSION ☐ A PRAISE

MY TAKEAWAY:	MY PRAYER:

READ: **MARK**
4:1-33

KNOW BEFORE YOU GO:

This chapter includes four parables, or stories, about people's possible responses to Jesus' teachings.

AFTER THE PASSAGE:

Mark 4 introduces us to one of Jesus' favorite teaching methods—parables. Parables are stories that use common, everyday images, like nature, family, or money, to explain a truth about God, salvation, or the Christian life. In Mark 4:1-20, Jesus uses a very familiar task to His audience, spreading seeds, to explain how different people respond to the Gospel. Some have no interest (the path in Mark 4:4, 15), some are interested at first but quickly lose focus (the rocky soil in Mark 4:5-6, 16-17), some lose faith after life becomes too difficult (the thorny soil in Mark 4:7, 18-19), and some fully accept the Gospel (the good soil in Mark 4:8, 20)!

Although most people typically focus on the different types of soil when they read Mark 4:1-20, maybe we should pay a little more attention to the role of the farmer. Regardless of the type of soil on which the seeds fall, the farmer's job is to keep throwing seed! In addition to a lesson about the hearts of people and their responses to the Gospel, this parable is a reminder that we should continuously share the Good News of Jesus with people—even if people do not always respond in the way that we hope. *Keep spreading the news about Jesus!* Just as the farmer cannot change the soil in the parable, we cannot control the hearts of those who hear the Gospel—only Jesus can. Our job is to keep spreading the news in the hopes that God will soften the hearts of those who hear it!

The parables that follow in this chapter (the lamp on a stand in Mark 4:21-25 and the mustard seed in Mark 4:30-34) further explain the parable of the sower. Our responsibility is to share the Good News of salvation, not "hide" or keep it to ourselves. As we spread the Good News, we never know how God may use that seed of truth in someone's life.

[THE BOTTOM LINE]

While we cannot control the condition of people's hearts, we can continue to tell people about Jesus.

EXPERIENCE

SHARE THE GOOD NEWS OF JESUS
WITH ONE PERSON TODAY

While this action can sometimes be scary, sharing the Good News of Jesus may be as simple as telling someone that you are reading your Bible and what you are learning. It may be praying with one of your friends or inviting them to come to church with you. Perhaps it is telling someone in your life, "God loves you and wants you to have a relationship with Him."

Remember, we are only responsible for throwing the seed!
Ask God to give you the courage to overcome any fears you may have.

[TAKEAWAY & PRAY]

MY PRAYER TODAY IS: ☐ A REQUEST ☐ A CONFESSION ☐ A PRAISE

MY TAKEAWAY:	MY PRAYER:

READ: **MARK**
4:35-41, 5:1-20

KNOW BEFORE YOU GO:

This next section of Mark continues to show that Jesus is not only a wise prophet or good teacher, but He is indeed God!

AFTER THE PASSAGE:

The story of the disciples in the boat is a reminder that even in the midst of life's storms, Jesus is present (Mark 4:35-41). The disciples are afraid—and they have every right to be! To be in the middle of a lake during a violent storm would be terrifying. What they do not realize, however, is that Jesus is God over everything—including creation and the weather! Despite their fear and lack of faith, Jesus delivers them from their near disaster (Mark 4:39). Interestingly, even after Jesus demonstrates His power over creation, the disciples are still unsure of who Jesus is and why He has such power (Mark 4:40-41).

When Jesus and the disciples safely arrive at the other side of the lake, they meet by a crazy, demon-possessed man—a man who is a danger to himself as well as the rest of the town (Mark 5:1-5). He is, in every sense of the word, out of control. As Jesus does in the previous story, He shows His control over creation and heals the man of his demon possession (Mark 5:13-15). For the second time in a matter of hours, Jesus brings order to chaos. He brings peace to a frightening situation!

Note: if this passage, or others about demon possession frighten you, take comfort in the fact that Jesus is way more powerful than the evil He faces in every scenario described in the Gospel of Mark. If you are following Jesus, there is no need to fear!

[THE BOTTOM LINE]

Jesus has the power to bring order to chaos.

EXPERIENCE

Illustrate what "chaos" looks like to you

Illustrate what "order" looks like to you

What is one area of your life that is in chaos to which you wish Jesus would bring order?
Pray and ask God for this peace.

[TAKEAWAY & PRAY]

MY PRAYER TODAY IS: ☐ A REQUEST ☐ A CONFESSION ☐ A PRAISE

MY TAKEAWAY:

MY PRAYER:

READ: MARK
5:21-43

KNOW BEFORE YOU GO:

This passage includes two miracles that Jesus performs in response to people's faith.

AFTER THE PASSAGE:

The story of Jairus' daughter and the sick woman is yet another powerful example of faith in the Gospel of Mark. The story begins with a religious man named Jairus who has tremendous faith. He truly believes that if Jesus was willing, He could heal his severely ill daughter (Mark 5:22-23). After agreeing to see Jairus' daughter, Jesus is interrupted by a sick woman who has similar faith to Jairus (Mark 5:25-28). She has been sick for over a decade and years of seeing doctors have not healed her. Despite her sickness, she believes Jesus has the power to heal her. In fact, her faith is so strong that just by touching Jesus' garment, her longtime illness is completely healed (Mark 5:34)!

While this reality is remarkable news for the sick woman, Jairus' daughter passes away while Jesus interacts with the woman. Hope is lost—Jairus' household thinks Jesus has not responded in time (Mark 5:35). Despite the seemingly hopeless situation, Jesus still travels to Jairus' house where his family and friends are mourning the passing of the young girl. In an incredible scene, Jesus brings the girl back to life—and orders her lunch (Mark 5:41-43)!

As we see in this passage, God's plan is often different than our plan. In the hearts and minds of everyone involved in this scene, Jesus is "too late" in His response to the people's needs. No one could have possibly blamed them for thinking this way—Jairus' daughter had passed away—they assumed it was final. Jesus, however, has another plan in mind. His plan involves an even more incredible display of power and healing, but His timeline is different than what the people expected.

Sometimes when we seek God, we need to remember He operates in His time according to His plan. God never forgets about you or runs late on accident—He has a purpose and appropriate time for everything. Accepting God's timing and plan, however, requires faith from us! We need to remember that no situation is ever hopeless. No matter what hardship you are facing, God is able to use any situation to show His power. Never give up faith!

[THE BOTTOM LINE]

God's plan and timing is perfect but often different than ours.

EXPERIENCE

What is one situation, person, or circumstance that you think God has "forgotten" about?

What do you wish God would do in this situation? Ask Him to do it today.

What can you learn about God or yourself as you wait for His response?

Pick a random time of day—any time. Maybe it is 8:12 or 10:10. Everyday at that time, remind yourself that God's timing is perfect.

[TAKEAWAY & PRAY]

MY PRAYER TODAY IS: ☐ A REQUEST   ☐ A CONFESSION   ☐ A PRAISE

| MY TAKEAWAY: | MY PRAYER: |

READ: # MARK
6:1-6,14-29

KNOW BEFORE YOU GO:

Jesus returns to His hometown and the people do not respond well.
Also, we sadly learn about the graphic death of John the Baptist.

AFTER THE PASSAGE:

The events in Mark 5 tell of two people, the sick woman and Jairus, who had never met Jesus but had complete faith in His power and ability to heal. The events in Mark 6 tell of people that flat out reject Jesus' words and miracles—the people in Jesus' hometown! These people knew Jesus as a young boy and were very familiar with His life story; yet, they are skeptical of His claims and power.

Mark 6:1-6 serve as a humble reminder that being *around* Jesus does not automatically result in belief, trust, and faith. The crowds in Jesus' hometown prove this truth—sometimes those most familiar with Jesus can miss the most important fact about Him: He is the Savior (Mark 6:4-6)! Knowledge of Jesus is dangerously different than faith in Jesus. Faith requires a response that knowledge does not. We sometimes dangerously assume being *around* Christian things, like church or Christian friends, will develop our faith for us.

It is appropriate to be a bit bothered by the story of John the Baptist's death in Mark 6:14-29. His beheading in the last part of this chapter is cruel, yet it serves as an example of how the message of Jesus often angers people (Mark 6:19-24). Two thousand years later, many people still struggle to understand and accept the words of Jesus; some may even find them offensive. Because of this reaction, we should not be surprised if we encounter opposition when we follow Jesus and actively put our faith in Him.

[THE BOTTOM LINE] ─────────────

Knowledge of Jesus is dangerously different than faith in Jesus.

EXPERIENCE

List the different things that people do if they are Christians.

Look back at your list. Which item guarantees salvation? Circle it.

To be honest, that last question was a bit of a trick question. The only thing that you can circle is *faith and trust in Jesus Christ*. All other actions are a result of that faith, not a substitute for it.

How do you keep a relationship with Jesus at the center of your actions?

If you have been relying on your Christian actions but never put your faith in Jesus, consider trusting Him with your life today. Take the time to pray this prayer or something like it, *"God, I understand that knowledge of you and faith in you are two different things. I want to put my faith in you and follow You each day of my life. Please forgive me of my sins. Thank you for offering salvation through Your Son, Jesus Christ. Help me understand what it means to keep You at the center of my actions each day."*

[TAKEAWAY & PRAY]

MY PRAYER TODAY IS: ☐ A REQUEST ☐ A CONFESSION ☐ A PRAISE

MY TAKEAWAY:

MY PRAYER:

READ: # MARK
6:30-56

KNOW BEFORE YOU GO:

This passage includes two of the most well-known stories of Jesus—the feeding of 5,000 and Jesus walking on water.

AFTER THE PASSAGE:

While much attention is rightly given to these miraculous acts, perhaps even more astounding is the care and compassion Jesus shows the people in these two miracles. In Mark 6:30-44, Jesus interacts with a crowd of people and notices their deeply spiritual needs. They are hurting. They are lost. They are in need of a leader. In response to their spiritual needs, Jesus feels compassion for them (Mark 6:34). *Perhaps this compassion is the reason for the miracle.* Jesus is able to meet their spiritual needs by first meeting their physical needs: lunch. If Jesus does not feed the crowd, the people will go home to eat and miss the opportunity to be with Jesus. Feeding the crowd lunch keeps them in Jesus' presence, and they therefore receive the love and care they need from their Shepherd.

Similarly, while Jesus is praying alone, He sees His disciples struggling in the middle of the sea. In another act of compassion and care, He walks out to them on the water and calms the sea (Mark 6:48). In both instances, the physical acts of Jesus are awesome—both miracles show His incredible power over the world He created. While we often focus on the miracles, do not miss the reason for them. It seems that Jesus' motivation behind both miracles is to show care and compassion to those around Him.

[THE BOTTOM LINE]

Jesus' compassion has no limits. Nothing can stop Jesus from loving us deeply!

Read Romans 8:38-39. What do these verses say about God's love for us?

Look in the mirror. How do you see yourself?
List the words that come to mind when you see the reflection looking back at you.

These two miracles remind us that Jesus not only sees us but loves us deeply. Write the numbers "6:34" and "6:48" on a sticky note and place it on your mirror. These two verses in Mark 6 tell us that Jesus sees and cares about His people. Let this sticky note serve as a reminder that Jesus sees you and cares about you!

[TAKEAWAY & PRAY]

MY PRAYER TODAY IS: ☐ A REQUEST ☐ A CONFESSION ☐ A PRAISE

MY TAKEAWAY:	MY PRAYER:

READ: **MARK** *7:1-23*

KNOW BEFORE YOU GO:

Jesus addresses another tradition from the Old Testament: people chose to ceremonially wash their hands before they ate in order to honor God. Jesus explains how this tradition has changed and also addresses an important truth.

AFTER THE PASSAGE:

The conversation about hand-washing between Jesus and the Pharisees in Mark 7 is not about germs or hygiene. The conversation centers around the way a person becomes holy in the eyes of God. These religious leaders had created an extra set of rules in order to protect themselves from breaking God's law. This ceremonial washing was a layer of protection from becoming unholy (Mark 7:3-5). While the heart behind these additional routines may have been pure at first, these "man made" rules eventually became just as important as God's original instructions (Mark 7:8). This shift is exactly what happened with the washing of hands. This washing was a tradition, or a preference, created by the Pharisees, not a commandment by God. Nonetheless, the religious leaders heavily judge and condemn those who do not follow their man made traditions of washing.

A modern day example of this tradition is the possible dress code of church. While there is nothing wrong with wearing nice clothes to church, nowhere in the Bible does God give us a dress code for worship. You can love God and wear shorts just as easily as you can wear nice clothes and have no relationship with Him (Mark 7:6-8). It would be wrong for you to judge someone for wearing shorts to church or to claim they are not a Christian because of their style of dress. This type of judgement would have been common of the Pharisees.

The issue with these types of traditions and preferences is that they are completely external and do not reflect the true condition of your heart. Jesus is more concerned about your heart and your resulting actions toward God and others (Mark 7:20-23).

[THE BOTTOM LINE]

Jesus cares deeply about the condition of our hearts.

EXPERIENCE

Make a timeline of your day yesterday.
Include some of your actions and interactions with others.

What was the motivation behind some of your actions yesterday? Did your actions stem from love, respect, or care for others? Or did they stem from selfishness, judgment, or anger?

Now, go wash your hands.
Every time you wash your hands today (which is hopefully a lot!), remind yourself that God is more concerned with the condition of your heart than He is with the condition of your hands. Each day is a new opportunity to understand this important truth.

[TAKEAWAY & PRAY]

MY PRAYER TODAY IS: ☐ A REQUEST ☐ A CONFESSION ☐ A PRAISE

MY TAKEAWAY:

MY PRAYER:

READ: # MARK
7:24-37

KNOW BEFORE YOU GO:

Jesus performs miracles on people who are often rejected and judged by the surrounding communities.

AFTER THE PASSAGE:

These two interactions once again show the compassion of Jesus—first to a non-Jewish woman (Mark 7:24-30) and second to a man who can neither hear or speak (Mark 7:31-37). Both of these individuals represent outcasts in Jewish society. The woman is Greek, or more importantly, not Jewish. She does not belong. Even as an outcast, she has faith—incredible faith! Jesus is amazed by her faith and therefore extends healing to her daughter (Mark 7:29-30). Similarly, in dramatic fashion, Jesus heals the deaf and mute man at the request of the man's friends (Mark 7:32-35).

Unfortunately, sometimes we think it is impossible for certain people to know Jesus. For one reason or another, we tend to assume that Jesus cares for a specific group of people. If we are honest with ourselves, this group of people look and act a lot like we do. Stories like Mark 7:24-37 remind us that Jesus is available to anyone who has faith. No one in your life, or in the entire world, is outside of the reach of Jesus! Regardless of a person's birth place, appearance, language, education, status, wealth, health, or even view of God, Jesus desires to have a relationship with everyone.

[THE BOTTOM LINE]

The Good News of Jesus is for everyone.

EXPERIENCE

Be like Jesus today and reach out to someone who seems to be an outsider. Talk to them, invite them to lunch with your friends, ask them some questions, and get to know them. Sometimes a simple act can go a long way to make someone feel loved!

As you reflect on this interaction, how were you like Jesus to this outsider today?

[TAKEAWAY & PRAY]

MY PRAYER TODAY IS: ☐ A REQUEST ☐ A CONFESSION ☐ A PRAISE

MY TAKEAWAY:	MY PRAYER:

READ: MARK 8:1-13

KNOW BEFORE YOU GO:

Once again, Jesus has compassion for a group of people—this time He feeds a crowd of 4,000 people who have been with Him for three days.

AFTER THE PASSAGE:

The situation is remarkably similar to the crowd of 5,000 mentioned in Mark 6. Unfortunately, the disciples react similarly as well. When the time comes to feed the crowd lunch, the disciples express the same concern as before. They ask Jesus how they can possibly feed such a massive crowd (Mark 8:4). While we do not know exactly how much time passed between these two miraculous feedings, the disciples could not have forgotten this previous miracle, could they? Where is the disciples' faith? Where is their confidence in Jesus' power that He has previously shown in this *exact same situation?*

While we are quick to mock the disciples for their lack of understanding, how often do we forget God's power in our own lives? Even after God shows Himself to be faithful to us, we start to doubt Him in our very next challenge. Remembering God's goodness in our past helps us have faith in our present circumstances. The disciples forget Jesus' power and ability to meet the very need He has previously met. The Pharisees also ask Jesus for a sign from heaven right after witnessing an amazing testament to His power (Mark 8:11-13). Both the disciples and the Pharisees need more assurance for their faith even though the faithfulness they experienced in their past should have been enough.

[THE BOTTOM LINE]

Remembering God's actions in the past is the key to our hope for the future.

EXPERIENCE

Make a list of the ways God has been faithful in your life. Consider previous doubts, fears, or worries you used to have.

In the past week...	In the past month...	In the past year...

How does remembering God's faithfulness in the past help you have faith for the future?

[TAKEAWAY & PRAY]

MY PRAYER TODAY IS: ☐ *A REQUEST* ☐ *A CONFESSION* ☐ *A PRAISE*

MY TAKEAWAY:	MY PRAYER:

READ: **MARK** 8:14-26

KNOW BEFORE YOU GO:

This passage includes a stern warning to the disciples to not follow the teachings of the Pharisees.

AFTER THE PASSAGE:

To serve as a reminder, the Pharisees are the religious leaders we discussed earlier in the Gospel of Mark. They are more concerned with rules and regulations than a relationship with God. In Mark 8:15, Jesus calls the Pharisees "yeast"—a powerful ingredient found in bread that makes it rise when baked. Just a small amount of yeast can completely change the makings of the bread. Jesus uses this image immediately after His miracle involving thousands of loaves of bread—this connection of yeast to loaves should help the disciples understand His warning. The teaching of the Pharisees is like yeast in bread, their thinking completely and wrongly changes how people interact with God.

The warning remains relevant for us today. Although the actual Pharisees no longer exist, there are certainly people in our lives who think like the Pharisees. These negative influences can be rather deceiving. At first glance, Pharisee-minded people seem very connected to God and His teachings. However, their commitment to religion only affects their actions and does not challenge their hearts. Pharisee-minded people can distract us from the heart of Jesus' teaching by tempting us to focus solely on the rules and traditions of religion. Pharisee-minded people miss the very point of the Gospel.

[THE BOTTOM LINE]

Our relationship with God can become distorted when we prioritize the motions over the motive.

EXPERIENCE

In Mark 8:22, Jesus meets a blind man from Bethsaida. This town is known for being a cruel and unwelcoming community. Like the Pharisees, they lack faith and doubt Jesus' power. Because of their thoughts toward Jesus, He chooses to heal the blind man outside of Bethsaida (Mark 8:23) and tells the man not to return to the village after Jesus heals him (Mark 8:26). Although this command from Jesus seems harsh, it illustrates how negative of an influence Pharisee-minded people can have on believers.

What or who in your life do you need to separate from to strengthen your relationship with God? This object, activity, or person may not be entirely bad, but its influence could be negatively impacting your life.

Pray to God and ask for clarity and strength as you consider separating yourself from this influence.

[TAKEAWAY & PRAY]

MY PRAYER TODAY IS: ☐ *A REQUEST*   ☐ *A CONFESSION*   ☐ *A PRAISE*

MY TAKEAWAY:	MY PRAYER:

READ: # MARK
8:27-33

KNOW BEFORE YOU GO:

These verses illustrate how Peter, a disciple of Jesus, understands Jesus' identity but not His significance as Savior.

AFTER THE PASSAGE:

As you can imagine, Jesus is extremely popular during His time on Earth. As He heals the sick, walks on water, and raises people from the dead, people start to notice Him. Furthermore, the message He preaches is different than the words of the religious leaders—and this difference is refreshing to hear.

His teachings and ministry make Jesus highly controversial. People have a difficult time drawing conclusions about His identity—who is Jesus? Is He a prophet like the prophets of the Old Testament (Mark 8:28)? Is He just a controversial Rabbi? Some think He is even crazy! Aware of this confusion around town, Jesus asks His disciples who *they* think He is. In other words, Jesus is asking His disciples to draw a conclusion for themselves.

Although we have seen the disciples stumble in the past, Peter has incredible faith and answers profoundly in this moment. He states that Jesus is the Messiah (Mark 8:29). However, Peter has yet to understand the significance of Jesus' *role* as the Messiah (Mark 8:32-33). He does not understand that Jesus' ministry on Earth is more than performing miracles and healing sick people—His role as the Messiah has the higher calling of the cross.

2,000 years laters, people still have all sorts of opinions about Jesus, but the question still remains for you personally: Who do you say Jesus is? This question is the most important question you could ever answer.

[THE BOTTOM LINE]

You must answer the question for yourself: "Who do you say I am?" (Mark 8:29).

EXPERIENCE

List some important people in your life. Who do they say Jesus is?

WHO DO YOU
SAY JESUS IS?

[TAKEAWAY & PRAY]

MY PRAYER TODAY IS: ☐ A REQUEST ☐ A CONFESSION ☐ A PRAISE

MY TAKEAWAY:	MY PRAYER:

READ: **MARK**
8:34-8:38, 9:1-9:29

KNOW BEFORE YOU GO:

Jesus explains the possible responses a person can have to the Gospel. Furthermore, Jesus shows three disciples His power through the Transfiguration. Finally, Jesus heals a possessed boy.

AFTER THE PASSAGE:

Although several interactions occur in these passages, the words of Jesus in Mark 8:34-8:38 and 9:1 are where we will focus our attention. Jesus' call to His people to "take up their cross" could define *how you live your entire life* (Mark 8:34).

As we read in Mark 8:29, Peter realizes that Jesus is the Messiah. Mark 8:34-8:38 and 9:1 then explains how we should respond to this reality. If we choose to believe that Jesus is the Messiah, then this choice requires a daily denial of ourselves, or to "take up our cross" (Mark 8:34). We lose our old life and exchange it for a new life (Mark 8:35). In other words, the person you were before you knew Jesus should be completely different than the person you are after choosing to follow Jesus.

The person you were before Jesus was first concerned about yourself—your comfort, your money, your relationships, and your status. Your focus was entirely on how you could become the greatest, wealthiest, and most successful person during your years on Earth. However, Jesus reminds us that gaining the whole world makes no difference if you have not decided to follow Jesus (Mark 8:36-38).

When you choose to follow Jesus, the focus of your life is now on Jesus. You are no longer focused on yourself, but rather focused on serving others, becoming humble, being generous, and showing others God's grace. Someone who truly follows Jesus realizes that this life on Earth is temporary, but the next life in Heaven is forever (Mark 8:35-36).

The statements Jesus makes at the end of this chapter should cause you to stop and reflect. If you have made the decision to follow Jesus, Mark 8:34-38 and 9:1 should motivate you to deny your old self daily and live according to Jesus' command. This choice may even cause you to make some sacrifices, but Jesus assures us that it is worth it in the end!

[THE BOTTOM LINE] ——————————————

Our life should be radically different when we decide to follow Jesus.

EXPERIENCE

Draw two people: one that represents your old life and one that represents your new life. Write ideas or things that each self prioritizes around each drawing. Consider what should be different about these two people. You may not remember your life before Jesus, so consider the difference between an Earthly focus and a Heavenly focus.

Old Self	New Self

What choices are you making to deny your old self and to focus your life on Jesus?

[TAKEAWAY & PRAY]

MY PRAYER TODAY IS: ☐ A REQUEST ☐ A CONFESSION ☐ A PRAISE

MY TAKEAWAY:

MY PRAYER:

READ: **MARK**
9:30-9:50

KNOW BEFORE YOU GO:

These passages include some bizarre instructions for followers of Jesus. The word pictures Jesus uses help us understand what Christians should prioritize in their walk with God.

AFTER THE PASSAGE:

Jesus' words at the end of Mark 9 are a great example of hyperbole. Hyperbole is when someone uses an extreme exaggeration to make a point. It would be like telling your mom after coming home from summer camp, "I am so tired I could sleep for days." You, of course, are not making a scientific claim about the number of hours you plan to rest, and your mom would certainly not expect you to sleep for 48 hours straight. While you are not necessarily using accurate details, you are being accurate in describing the principle—you are extremely exhausted. If you said, "Summer camp was a lot of fun—I am pretty tired," your mom may not have fully understood just how tired you were. By saying, "I could sleep for days," she now knows not to plan any family dinners or activities because you need some serious rest!

Jesus uses this type of speech in His teaching on temptation and sin in Mark 9:42-50. His point is not to start chopping off body parts; rather, Jesus further illustrates that the things of this world are temporary and worth far less than our souls (as we just read in Mark 8:34-38 and 9:1). In other words, it is better to limp after Jesus than run after the world. If something is hurting our relationship with Jesus, we should do whatever we can to get rid of it—even if it requires extreme action!

[THE BOTTOM LINE]

Our relationship with Jesus is valuable and worth protecting at all costs.

EXPERIENCE

Many things can hurt our relationship with Jesus. Certain things tempt us and lead us into a pattern of sin. Some things distract us by taking up too much time in our schedules. Others, even if they are good things, become too big of a priority in our lives. All of these things, even if for different reasons, can impact our relationship with Jesus.

What are some of these things for you?

What are some "extreme" ways to handle them and what are some realistic ways to handle them?

Things that hurt my relationship with Jesus	"Hyperbole" Solution	Practical Solution
My TV	Throw my TV off the roof	Limit the amount of time I watch TV

[TAKEAWAY & PRAY]

MY PRAYER TODAY IS: ☐ *A REQUEST*   ☐ *A CONFESSION*   ☐ *A PRAISE*

MY TAKEAWAY:

MY PRAYER:

READ: MARK 10:1-31

KNOW BEFORE YOU GO:

Jesus interacts with several people who are familiar with the Old Testament law. He challenges their interpretations of this law and how the Gospel changes the law's application.

AFTER THE PASSAGE:

Jesus' interaction with the rich man in Mark 10:17-31 continues to highlight the theme that we see in the Gospel of Mark: nothing on this Earth is worth more than a relationship with Jesus. Do you remember some of the other examples of this theme? Jesus tells His disciples that following Him means that they are to "take up their cross daily" and asks them the thought-provoking question, "What good is it if you gain the whole world but lose your soul?" (Mark 8:36). Later, He explains that even our hands, feet, and eyes are not worth more than following Jesus (Mark 9:42-50).

In Mark 10:20, the rich man tells Jesus that he has kept every commandment from the Old Testament. This feat is highly unlikely—no one could keep the entire law. Jesus does not confront the rich man's obvious lie. Rather, Jesus suggests a rather bold action to expose the condition of the rich man's heart: Jesus tells him to sell everything and then follow Him (Mark 10:21). The man's reaction reveals exactly what Jesus is trying to explain. He follows the rules to gain wealth and influence on Earth, not to experience a relationship with God.

The rich man leaves Jesus without understanding Jesus' point (Mark 10:22). Jesus then explains to His disciples that the rich have a hard time seeing their need for Jesus because wealth meets most of their physical needs (Mark 10:23-25). Money or stuff is not evil; however, it can distract us from seeing that Jesus is the most important thing in life and the only way to meet our greater, spiritual needs (Mark 10:27-31).

Are Jesus' instructions to the rich man the same instructions to us? Are we suppose to sell everything in order to follow Jesus? Not necessarily. His instructions to the man are to expose that the man's heart is far from God and far too attached to this world. While Jesus' instructions are not exactly meant for us, the principle behind His question still applies to us. Is our priority this world or Jesus?

[THE BOTTOM LINE]

Jesus should be our number one priority in life.

EXPERIENCE

For the rich man, money was the object that he put above a relationship with Jesus. While it may not be money for you, there are likely a few things in your life that you are tempted to love more than Jesus.

Illustrate three things in your life that would be hard for you to "give up" if Jesus commanded you to.

Watch out for these things! While these things are likely not bad, they may become more important than Jesus if you are not careful.

[TAKEAWAY & PRAY]

MY PRAYER TODAY IS: ☐ *A REQUEST*   ☐ *A CONFESSION*   ☐ *A PRAISE*

MY TAKEAWAY:	MY PRAYER:

READ: **MARK** 10:32-52

KNOW BEFORE YOU GO:

Jesus cares for His, at times selfish, disciples by predicting His upcoming death and explaining the importance of service. He also heals a blind man who is overlooked by many.

AFTER THE PASSAGE:

The disciples are often slow in their understanding of Jesus' messages. For example, in Mark 10:31, Jesus tells His disciples "the first shall be last" in the Kingdom of God. What happens just a few verses later? The disciples start arguing about who will be first and who will get to be the most powerful person in heaven (Mark 10:37)! The disciples clearly misunderstand the mission of Jesus—which is to promote the Kingdom of God, not to make people powerful.

When Jesus says, "The first shall be last and the last shall be first," He is not saying that everyone who has ever been last in line will be first in line in Heaven. Jesus simply means the Gospel changes everything. Everything we value on Earth does not matter when it comes to following Jesus—He turns our Earthly priorities upside down. The world values being strong, Jesus values acknowledging our weakness. The world values being rich, Jesus values removing distractions. The world values popularity, Jesus values everyone knowing His name. The world values selfish power, Jesus values humble service. Jesus changes everything. Our mission in life does not center around ourselves; it centers around Jesus and pointing people to Him as we serve others (Mark 10:42-45).

In Mark 10:51, Jesus asks the blind man, Bartimaeus, "What do you want me to do for you?" He asks this same question to the disciples in Mark 10:36. The disciples answer, "We want you to make us great" and Jesus does not grant their request. The blind man, however, simply answers, "I want to see" and Jesus heals the man. The different answers to the same question serve as yet another example of Jesus' radical priorities: Jesus models His commandment and serves the blind, poor, beggar (Mark 10:52). The request of His disciples to be great simply does not align with Jesus' mission on Earth!

[THE BOTTOM LINE] ———————————————

The most powerful people in the kingdom of God are humble servants.

EXPERIENCE

1 *SERVE*
SOMEONE TODAY

2 *MEMORIZE*
MARK 10:45

[**TAKEAWAY & PRAY**]

MY PRAYER TODAY IS: ☐ A REQUEST ☐ A CONFESSION ☐ A PRAISE

| MY TAKEAWAY: | MY PRAYER: |

READ: MARK
11:1-11

KNOW BEFORE YOU GO:

In ancient times, a king's grand entrance into the temple was a very important moment because the temple was the most important building in town. In this passage, we experience Jesus' entry into the temple of Jerusalem.

AFTER THE PASSAGE:

The events in these verses take place a week before Easter—the Sunday typically known as Palm Sunday. Jesus is at the height of His popularity—everyone in town knows of His teachings and miracles. When word spreads that Jesus is coming to town to celebrate the Jewish holidays, crowds start to form in order to get a glimpse of Jesus. When Jesus walks by, the crowds yell, "Hosanna," which is a word used to worship a Savior (Mark 11:9-10). They indeed believe that Jesus is going to be their Savior; however, the crowds do not understand *how and from what* Jesus is going to save them. The expectation of the crowds is that Jesus is going to do something extraordinary in the coming week—perhaps even lead a revolution to take back their city from the Romans!

We see multiple times in the Gospel of Mark that Jesus challenges the way people think about everything. Though He is as popular as ever, He does not use a chariot with majestic stallions and musicians. He rides into town on a borrowed donkey (Mark 11:2, 7). And when He finally arrives at His destination, the temple, nothing happens. No rally. No speech. He simply turns around and goes home.

This humble entrance should have alerted the crowds that Jesus is not going to start the revolution they want. Jesus is the Savior from their sin, but not from the Roman government. Jesus' death on a cross, just a week after His humble entrance into the city, is infinitely better than anything the crowds could have hoped for. Unfortunately, the crowds do not understand this truth, and they abandon Jesus in the coming days.

[*THE BOTTOM LINE*] ────────────────

Jesus' plan can exceed our most hopeful expectations.

EXPERIENCE

What are some of your biggest hopes? For your life? For your family? For your friends?

If your hopes become your reality, how would your life change?

Now dream with Jesus in mind. How can Jesus transform your hopes to show people His power?

[TAKEAWAY & PRAY]

MY PRAYER TODAY IS: ☐ A REQUEST ☐ A CONFESSION ☐ A PRAISE

MY TAKEAWAY:	MY PRAYER:

READ: **MARK**

11:12-11:33, 12:1-12

KNOW BEFORE YOU GO:

During Jesus' time in Jerusalem, He faces opposition. First, He rebukes the religious leaders for making the temple a marketplace and challenges their unbelief. Then, He tells a parable that foreshadows their rejection of Jesus as the Son of God.

AFTER THE PASSAGE:

A day after Jesus' celebratory entrance into the city (Mark 11:1-11), Jesus rebukes the money changers in the temple courts who are profiting from people's worship experiences (Mark 11:15-18). The money changers are charging people for the animal they need to sacrifice to God in the temple. This scam is like paying $10 for a toothbrush at the airport. A toothbrush does not cost $10, but airport vendors take advantage of your forgetfulness and now limited options. However, the money changers' upcharge is a much worse scam because they are making money off of God's commands to worship Him at the temple! Jesus' anger is righteous!

Jesus' interactions in Mark 11 and 12 are the final straw for the religious leaders. For many months, the religious leaders are frustrated by Jesus' teaching and the popularity of His message (Mark 11:18). Jesus' message is not only a different message, but it actually calls their teaching wrong (Mark 12:12). For generations, these religious leaders have been the spiritual authority for their people. They were the ones who told people what rules to follow and how to interact with God.

Understandably, the religious leaders feel incredibly threatened. The new message of Jesus makes them less powerful, important, and influential. Their solution is to eliminate Jesus by killing Him in hopes of stopping His message. The parable in Mark 12:1-12 is Jesus' sharp warning to the Pharisees who are planning to kill Him. Jesus references the Old Testament as well, showing the religious leaders that He Himself is the cornerstone of the Christian faith (Mark 12:10-11). Rather than listening to the warning and believing Jesus, the religious leaders grow more angry (Mark 12:12).

[THE BOTTOM LINE]

Jesus' message of truth can be controversial.

EXPERIENCE

Look through your music and pick your five favorite songs. What advice are the song lyrics telling you as the listener? List the songs' messages below.

Are the messages similar to Jesus' message of truth? Why or why not?

Be aware of the messages you are allowing to inform your life.

[TAKEAWAY & PRAY]

MY PRAYER TODAY IS: ☐ *A REQUEST*   ☐ *A CONFESSION*   ☐ *A PRAISE*

MY TAKEAWAY:

MY PRAYER:

READ: **MARK**
12:13-34

KNOW BEFORE YOU GO:

The religious leaders try to trick Jesus. They ask Him questions from three categories: tax laws, marriage laws, and Old Testament laws. If Jesus answers incorrectly to their questions, then they can discredit His message.

AFTER THE PASSAGE:

Not only do the religious leaders ignore Jesus' warning in the previous parable (Mark 12:1-12), they make a plan to trick Jesus into saying something that would upset the crowds and politicians of the day (Mark 12:13). They think if they can get Jesus to say something wrong, then they can turn people against Jesus. The problem with this plan? Jesus is infinitely wise and knowledgeable. Every time they try to trick Him, Jesus gives a perfect and astounding answer to their questions.

Perhaps the most significant answer occurs when the Pharisees ask the question, "Which commandment is most important?" (Mark 12:28). The ultimate trick question! There were literally hundreds of commandments in the Old Testament—how could Jesus pick one over the others? If He picks one commandment, then He ignores the rest of God's Old Testament law. Rather than pick a specific commandment, Jesus recites a line that would have been very familiar to a Jewish person in His time: Deuteronomy 6:4-5, a passage known as *The Shema* (Mark 12:29-31). It serves as a great reminder to the Jewish people of who God is and His expectations for His people. When Jesus references this line as a response to their question, He essentially concludes that the most important law is not actually a law at all—it is to love God (Mark 12:29-30). He continues by saying that loving your neighbor is the second greatest commandment (Mark 12:31). With these two instructions, Jesus summarizes the entire law into two simple truths, and everyone listening is amazed (Mark 12:32-34).

[THE BOTTOM LINE] ————————————————

Love God. Love others.

EXPERIENCE

Find a coin.

Every coin has two sides: heads and tails. You cannot have a coin without both sides—a one sided coin simply does not exist! Jesus' command to love God and love others is like the two sides of the "following God coin." You have to love both to truly follow God.

Every time you see a coin, think about the heads side as "loving God" and the tails side as "loving others."

How can you love God today?

How can you love others today?

[TAKEAWAY & PRAY]

MY PRAYER TODAY IS: ☐ *A REQUEST* ☐ *A CONFESSION* ☐ *A PRAISE*

MY TAKEAWAY:

MY PRAYER:

READ: # MARK

12:35-44

KNOW BEFORE YOU GO:

Jesus continues to teach at the temple and challenge the religious leaders' conclusions and values.

AFTER THE PASSAGE:

The widow's offering in Mark 12:41-44 serves as another example of Jesus' counter-cultural values. The wealthy give significantly more money than the woman (Mark 12:41). To understand their giving in modern day amounts, the wealthy give around $100 and the woman gives 25 cents. Despite the large contributions of many wealthy individuals, Jesus proclaims that the incredibly small gift from the widow is the most generous gift of that day (Mark 12:43). In what world is a quarter worth more than $100?

In Jesus' world, He is far more concerned with the condition of our hearts than the value of our stuff. Jesus repeatedly reminds His disciples that the first shall be last. While the amount of the widow's offering is quite small, it is *everything* she has. She selflessly gives her resources to bless others and obey God. Her heart is pure and others-focused. The rich selfishly give only a small fraction of their fortune. Their hearts are hard and selfish.

This small scene also reinforces Jesus' instructions to not prioritize the wealth, stuff, and distractions of this world over a relationship with God. The heart of the widow contrasts the heart of the rich man that Jesus meets in Mark 10. That rich man cannot imagine giving up his possessions to have a relationship with God. This widow voluntarily gives all she has out of obedience and love for God!

[THE BOTTOM LINE] ─────────────

True generosity reflects the condition of our hearts rather than the value of our giving.

EXPERIENCE

BE GENEROUS
TO SOMEONE TODAY

It may mean buying someone lunch, it may mean giving away your hard-earned allowance, or it may mean sharing your favorite thing with someone else.

[TAKEAWAY & PRAY]

MY PRAYER TODAY IS: ☐ A REQUEST ☐ A CONFESSION ☐ A PRAISE

MY TAKEAWAY:	MY PRAYER:

READ: # MARK
13:1-37

KNOW BEFORE YOU GO:

This chapter includes more serious content: Jesus discusses the end of this world and the coming of His Kingdom.

AFTER THE PASSAGE:

For those interested with the end times, Mark 13 is a jackpot! This chapter includes all sorts of warnings, signs, and end times language. But for most people, the chapter is confusing, a bit scary, and seemingly lacks any sort of practical applications.

While Jesus' teaching in Mark 13 is certainly fascinating, we sometimes overcomplicate this passage by trying interpret Jesus' words in a way that He never intends for us to do. For instance, some teachers may try to use these words to help determine exactly what the end of the Earth will look like, what will happen, when it will happen, and how it will happen. The problem with this approach is that Jesus does not want us to draw those conclusions from this text.

So, if Jesus is not trying to give us an exact end-times timeline, what is He trying to do? Do you notice any themes or repeated words in His sermon? Look for words like "Watch out" and "Be on guard" (Mark 13:5, 9, 23, 33-37). It seems that Jesus is trying to appeal to our hearts rather than teach end-times theology. He warns us to stay pure, avoid temptation, and be aware that He can come back at any time. We need to avoid the pressure of this world and not compromise what we believe about God.

Hundreds of generations have come and gone without Jesus returning or the world ending. The question we need to ask ourselves is, "Am I ready for Jesus to come back?" not "Will Jesus come back in my lifetime?" We need to stand firm in our faith for Jesus and watch out for those things that can turn us away.

[THE BOTTOM LINE]

We should be ready for Jesus to return at any time.

EXPERIENCE

This passage is not meant to scare us or help us "predict" Jesus' return. Instead, this passage should urge us to live our lives as if Jesus was coming back tomorrow!

What is one change you would want to make in your life today if you knew Jesus was coming back tomorrow?

[TAKEAWAY & PRAY]

MY PRAYER TODAY IS: ☐ A REQUEST ☐ A CONFESSION ☐ A PRAISE

MY TAKEAWAY:	MY PRAYER:

READ: # MARK
14:1-26

KNOW BEFORE YOU GO:

Jesus interacts with another poor woman who selflessly serves Him. Then, Jesus shares the Last Supper meal with His disciples, predicts His betrayal, and offers the first Communion.

AFTER THE PASSAGE:

In Jesus' final meal with His disciples, He shares some disturbing news: one of His disciples is going to betray Him (Mark 14:18). Look carefully at how the disciples respond to this sad revelation. They do not question Jesus, they do not mourn the news, and they do not ask how they could help stop the betrayal. The disciples' first reaction is worry! They each ask Jesus if they are the ones to betray Him (Mark 14:19)!

This reaction shows the insecurity, and perhaps the doubt, that the disciples still have about following Jesus. Even after years of hearing His teachings and witnessing His miracles, there still seems to be a hint of nervousness around whether or not they are fully committed to following Jesus.

Your commitment to Jesus must be a personal choice. Judas, the disciple that ultimately betrays Jesus, is further proof that being around the "right" group of people does not guarantee a personal relationship with Jesus. Christian friends, parents, and teachers are certainly encouraging and beneficial, but each person is responsible to make independent choices. While the other disciples have their moments of doubt, their personal beliefs and convictions allow them to stay faithful to Jesus. The meal Jesus shares with His disciples in Mark 14:22-25 is the spiritual practice of Communion that we can still exercise today. It helps remind us to choose Jesus and reflect on His sacrifice for us.

[THE BOTTOM LINE]

Your choice to follow Jesus must be a personal decision that affects every part of your life.

EXPERIENCE

When are you tempted to hide your faith in God?

When is it easier to pretend that you do not know God or care about what the Bible says?

Write out a prayer to God asking Him to give you the strength to choose God each day. Ask for the strength to not deny Him and rely on yourself in difficult situations.

[TAKEAWAY & PRAY]

MY PRAYER TODAY IS: ☐ A REQUEST   ☐ A CONFESSION   ☐ A PRAISE

MY TAKEAWAY:

MY PRAYER:

READ: MARK
14:27-73

KNOW BEFORE YOU GO:

These verses begin the story of Jesus' death. First, Jesus predicts that His disciple, Peter, will deny Him, which Peter does several days later. Jesus is also arrested in Gethsemane and put on trial by the religious leaders.

AFTER THE PASSAGE:

Jesus' prayer in the Garden of Gethsemane shows the depth of His pain and sorrow (Mark 14:34-36). In most of Jesus' interactions, we see that He is God—He performs miracles and teaches with amazing authority. In this scene, however, we see that Jesus is also fully human. Like any other human, Jesus is hurting and feels deep sorrow for what is to come. He is fully aware of the awful things that await Him in the next few days, and it is His deep desire to avoid them if at all possible. Amazingly enough, Jesus prays that He will do whatever God wants! Even in His pain and sorrow, Jesus provides an amazing example of someone who trusts in God's plan no matter the cost.

After His arrest in Gethsemane, Jesus is brought before a Jewish court (Mark 14:43-65). Even after His arrest and trial, the religious leaders are unable to prove Jesus has done anything wrong! Finally, when they directly ask Jesus if He is the Son of God, He replies truthfully, "I am" (Mark 14:61-62). If someone had falsely claimed to be the Son of God, the Jewish people had the right to punish this person. However, *Jesus is the Son of God*. Nevertheless, the court does not believe His claim and finds Jesus guilty of lying! In Mark 14:66-72, Peter also fails to recognize Jesus' true identity. Even though Peter believes Jesus to be the Son of God, his current fear and worry causes him to deny His Savior.

As we learn from these interactions in Mark 14, what we believe about Jesus is incredibly important! Do you believe He is God? Do you trust Him no matter what? Do you think He is a liar pretending to be God's son? Do you doubt Him in times of stress?

[THE BOTTOM LINE]

Jesus loves us despite our reactions to Him.

EXPERIENCE

For an entire day, keep track of how many times you hear the word "love."
What are some things we typically say we love?

How is the love that Jesus displays for us different than other types of love?

WHAT IS YOUR RESPONSE
TO JESUS' LOVE?

[TAKEAWAY & PRAY]

MY PRAYER TODAY IS: ☐ A REQUEST   ☐ A CONFESSION   ☐ A PRAISE

MY TAKEAWAY:

MY PRAYER:

READ: **MARK**
15:1-20

KNOW BEFORE YOU GO:

Sentencing Jesus to death is a very final decision. The religious leaders continue to look for someone who can make this decision with certainty. Unable to do so, the Roman leader, Pilate, transfers Barabbas' status of a criminal onto Jesus.

AFTER THE PASSAGE:

After Jesus' appearance before the Jewish court, He goes before the Roman government and meets a man named Pilate (Mark 15:1). Pilate experiences the same problem the religious leaders experienced in court the night before: Pilate is unable to find Jesus guilty.

Although Pilate knows Jesus is innocent, Pilate lets fear direct his decision. Pilate fears what the crowd will think of him if he does not hand Jesus over to be crucified. The people want Jesus dead (Mark 15:10-15), and the politician in Pilate cares more about his position of power than protecting the truth. Pilate chooses to release a man named Barabbas, a convicted criminal who actually deserves to be in jail, and lets the religious leaders continue their plan to kill Jesus (Mark 15:15).

While this decision to transfer Barabbas' punishment onto Jesus is incredibly unfair, it is a picture of why Jesus came to Earth: to set the prisoner free and forgive the guilty. Barabbas does not deserve to be set free; he should pay the penalty for his sins. Yet, because Jesus takes his place as a prisoner, Barabbas is able to have a new life. We too are guilty of doing wrong and sinning. We too are lost without Jesus. And we too can be set free and have a new life because of Jesus' perfect sacrifice! In some ways, Barabbas is the first to experience the grace of the cross!

[THE BOTTOM LINE]

Jesus saves us from the punishment we deserve by taking it upon Himself.

EXPERIENCE

Think of a time that you gave grace to a person who did not deserve it. What was it?

Think of a time you received grace that you did not deserve. What was it?

How did you feel during both of these interactions?

Spend a few minutes thanking Jesus for giving you the grace that you do not deserve.

[TAKEAWAY & PRAY]

MY PRAYER TODAY IS: ☐ A REQUEST ☐ A CONFESSION ☐ A PRAISE

MY TAKEAWAY:	MY PRAYER:

READ: # MARK
15:21-47

KNOW BEFORE YOU GO:

This passage describes the pain and suffering Jesus experiences during His crucifixion. Jesus' body is then buried in a tomb nearby.

AFTER THE PASSAGE:

Over the past few chapters of Mark, you read about the brutal torture Jesus endured in the final days of His life. The beatings, insults, and mockery ultimately lead to death by crucifixion. Crucifixion is an incredibly painful and humiliating way to die. It is a punishment reserved for the worst of the worst because of its severity. Why does Jesus have to die this way?

Simply put, Jesus' crucifixion shows us the severity of our sin, the extent of Jesus' humility, and the depth of His love for us. If Jesus is to pay the ultimate price for our sins, He needs to actually pay the price. The punishment for a criminal is to be whipped, beaten, and killed. Even though Jesus has never sinned and is perfectly holy, He takes on the punishment completely. Jesus' crucifixion serves as the ultimate example of humility and love.

Finally, it proves how much God loves us. Jesus endures such suffering to have a relationship with us. When Jesus finally dies, an incredible miracle happens in the temple (Mark 15:37-39). There was a large curtain that divided the common places of the temple from the Holy of Holies, a space where God's spirit dwelled. Only the high priest could enter the Holy of Holies, and the curtain served as a stopping point for everyone else. In Mark 15:38, God tears the curtain in half from top to bottom. This tear is incredibly symbolic—everyone can now interact with God. We are not limited or restricted, we are free from sin, and we are free to experience a relationship with God through Jesus' death on the cross!

[THE BOTTOM LINE]

While brutal to read, the crucifixion is how we can understand Jesus' mission, His love for us, and the gift of salvation!

EXPERIENCE

The cross has been a symbol of Christianity for 2,000 years. For some people, the cross is just a nice piece of jewelry or an interesting thing to put on a wall. For others, the cross is a great reminder of how much Jesus loves them. How many crosses do you see in an average week? (It would be interesting to actually keep track!)

The cross is a reminder that Jesus loves you. When you see a cross, think of Jesus literally saying, "I love you." When you see a cross, pray the words, "I love you too" back to Jesus to continually remind yourself of the love displayed by the cross.

**CROSS
= I LOVE YOU**

[*TAKEAWAY & PRAY*]

MY PRAYER TODAY IS: ☐ *A REQUEST*   ☐ *A CONFESSION*   ☐ *A PRAISE*

MY TAKEAWAY:	*MY PRAYER:*

READ: # MARK
16:1-8

KNOW BEFORE YOU GO:

Three days later, Mary Magdalene discovers that Jesus' tomb is empty. Jesus has risen from the dead and is alive!

AFTER THE PASSAGE:

The hours following Jesus' death had to be some of the most confusing and depressing hours in all of human history. For those that followed Jesus and believed Him to be the Son of God, His death must have shattered their hopes and expectations. As we learn in Mark 11, the people think Jesus is going to save them from their current Roman rulers. It seems as though they have placed their hope in the wrong person. It seems as though the religious leaders who opposed Jesus were in fact correct: Jesus' death must have meant that He was a fraud because the Son of God should not die. Jesus' disciples must have asked themselves, "Should we still follow Jesus' teachings or go back to believing the Pharisees?"

It is hard to imagine the sadness, frustration, and disappointment that those closest to Jesus must have felt when Jesus died because we know the ending—we know that Jesus does not stay dead! The fact that Jesus rises from the dead validates everything He says He is! His resurrection is the ultimate proof that He is the Son of God. The women's fearful reaction in Mark 16:8 is incredibly understandable—Jesus conquered death! Amazing!

For a follower of Jesus, there are no sweeter words than, "He is risen. He is not here!" (Mark 16:6). It is the resurrection of Jesus that gives us hope. It is the reason we can have confidence in our faith. It is why we can read a Gospel like Mark and try our best to put Jesus' words into practice. His resurrection proves that Jesus' teachings are true and worth following!

[THE BOTTOM LINE]

Jesus is alive and is the Savior of the world!

EXPERIENCE

What are some of your doubts about God?

Sometimes doubting can force us to ask healthy questions about our faith.

Who in your life can help you process some of these questions or doubts?

Is Jesus the Savior of your life? Write a prayer that reflects the answer to this question.

[TAKEAWAY & PRAY]

MY PRAYER TODAY IS: ☐ *A REQUEST* ☐ *A CONFESSION* ☐ *A PRAISE*

MY TAKEAWAY:

MY PRAYER:

READ: **MARK**

16:9-20

KNOW BEFORE YOU GO:

Most likely, your Bible says something like, "The earliest manuscripts do not include verses 9-20." This note simply means that it is hard to tell exactly where these verses come from—the original author, Mark, or authors later in the process. Nevertheless, we can still learn from these verses as they include Jesus' instructions to His disciples before He returns to Heaven.

AFTER THE PASSAGE:

At the end of the Gospel of Mark, Jesus shows Himself to be the Son of God. He meets with Mary and the disciples, and He restores their faith in Him (Mark 16:9-14).

In His final moments on Earth, Jesus instructs the disciples to spread His message and teachings to the far corners of the Earth (Mark 16:15). And they do (Mark 16:20)! Through the power of God, they change the future of the world in Jesus' name. The fact that we are still talking about Jesus all over the world today is evidence of the disciples' obedience to Jesus' instructions!

We have come to the end of the Gospel of Mark. The teachings of Jesus recorded in this Gospel are not just stories, they are the actual events of God's Son. The message is true and directly from the mouth of God. This Gospel shows us a better way to live. This Gospel turns our world upside down and sets our priorities on spiritual things rather than physical things. Remember, you must personally answer the question, "Who is Jesus?" Your answer is the most important thing in your life.

[THE BOTTOM LINE] ————————————————

Tell everyone you meet about Jesus and what He means to you!

EXPERIENCE

Take a moment to reflect on your accomplishment. You have now read the entire Gospel of Mark!

What is one thing you learned from reading the Gospel of Mark?

What is one way you will now think of Jesus differently?

What is one way you will now act differently?

[TAKEAWAY & PRAY]

MY PRAYER TODAY IS: ☐ A REQUEST ☐ A CONFESSION ☐ A PRAISE

MY TAKEAWAY:

MY PRAYER:

EXPERIENCE THE WISDOM OF

PROVERBS

A 31 DAY JOURNEY THROUGH GOD'S WORD

EXPERIENCE
SCRIPTURE
STUDENTS

EXPERIENCE SCRIPTURE

Do you believe students can read and understand the Bible by themselves? We do! Experience Scripture is designed specifically to help students engage with God's Word through reading and reflection. It is our prayer that students will apply the principles revealed in Scripture as they seek to better understand God and His plan for their life.

EXPERIENCE SCRIPTURE IS:

ROOTED IN SCRIPTURE:
Our desire is to help students develop a life-long love and understanding of Scripture. While we hope they enjoy our book, we are more interested in empowering students to see the wisdom, practicality, and depth of God's Word.

BEAUTIFULLY DESIGNED:
We have worked hard to ensure that students will be proud of the look and feel of this book. Our design promotes authentic and thoughtful engagement with scripture.

ACCESSIBLE:
Our resources are meant to be completed in one month. Additionally, each day includes a brief explanation the passage's major themes to help students understand Scripture.

EXPERIMENTAL:
We believe Scripture is meant to be experienced, not just read. Our resources provide tangible ways for students to interact with the truth of Scripture.

@xpscripture

XPSCRIPTURE.COM

ISBN 978-3-16-148410-0

EXPERIENCE THE LETTERS OF

JAMES&JOHN

A 30 DAY JOURNEY THROUGH GOD'S WORD

EXPERIENCE
SCRIPTURE
STUDENTS

Made in the USA
Monee, IL
20 February 2023

28264805R00040